Focus on the

and Win the Game of Life

Focus on the

Final Seconds

and Win the Game of Life

Almon Gunter

Published by Advantage, Charleston, South Carolina.
Member of Advantage Media Group.

ADVANTAGE is a registered trademark and the
Advantage colophon is a trademark of Advantage Media Group, Inc.

Printed in the United States of America

First Printing: July 2006
ISBN: 1-59932-026-6

This book is dedicated to everyone who has a passion for life – those of you who strive to make the world a better place. In refusing to settle for mediocrity, you raise the bar so each of us may achieve our full potential.

You do not quit or give up on the game of life. In listening and paying close attention to others, you improve the world by being a part of it.

I thank you for your leadership, your undying spirit, and for the positive energy you bring to the game every day. May this book give you one more reason to land among the stars, one more reason to care about others, and one more reason to keep playing the game of life. I appreciate each of you.

Beyond a shadow of a doubt, together, we will win!

Almon W. Gunter, Jr.
CEO/President Gunter-Gunter, Inc.

I WILL WIN

By Almon Gunter

I will win because I know respect,
I will win because I know responsibility,
I will win because I am smart,
I will win because I am free,
I will win because I am committed,
I will win because I know sacrifice,
I will win because I know preparation,
I will win because I believe I will,
And though I respect your opinion of me
It's my opinion of me that matters most
That's why I know I will win!

Table of Contents

Foreword

In this book, Almon provides a fusion of material, spanning personal accounts, professional training, and competitions. Focusing on the individual as well as groups, he addresses students, parents, employees, and employers, all having a variety of interests and needs.

Begin these pages as if you have never read any other book like it. Probably, you are acquainted with setting goals and making plans to achieve your goals. But have you visualized the final results? Have you seen yourself hitting your mark? Have you seen yourself doing the work necessary to achieve your goals?

Visualizing your destination and doing the work are key in winning the game of life. To assure a successful outcome, Almon gives you a formula. Although no math is required, it involves proper planning, overcoming difficult issues with honesty, and engaging in positive actions. If you are not honest, the formula breaks down and the outcome cannot be favorable. With honesty, greatness will happen.

To assist you in winning the game, Almon tells incredible stories associated with his simple life instructions. His book provides a unique and failsafe approach for achieving your desires, whether you aspire to become the best student, athlete, or CEO. In Focus on the Final Seconds!™ you'll learn how to make a plan, do the work, and see yourself winning. Almon Gunter will help you bring your dreams to life.

Foreword written by Yvette Arline

INTRODUCTION

This book is the result of two of my greatest loves: the love for my grandfather and the love for competing in track and field. Both gave me the life skills and tools I needed to win the most important game of all, the game of life. They shaped my character and molded me into a champion, on and off the track.

After many years of dreaming about sharing these loves with the world, I decided to wake up and do it. Malcolm X once said, "If you are dreaming you are sleeping, you must wake up and put forth a positive effort to make your dreams a reality." ***Focus on the Final Seconds!***™ became a reality.

My grandfather, Wilson Gunter, was one of the most influential people in my life. If I were to put into print all of the things he taught me, I would have to write another book. A remarkable man, my grandfather believed in hard work, self-discipline, and living life to its fullest each and every day. He used to say, ***"Son, every day you wake up is another opportunity to achieve greatness."*** You will read many quotes from my grandfather throughout this book. The quotes are all in quotations and italics just like the previous one above, so you can easily identify them. I hope after reading his quotations, you will be inspired as I was, to be the best at whatever you decide to do.

Among the many lessons my grandfather taught me, two stand out the most – his two R's: respect and responsibility. His philosophy of life was simple: what you get out of life is directly proportionate to what you put into it. If you do nothing or risk nothing, you get nothing.

Respect.

You must respect yourself first before you can respect others. When you look in the mirror, you must like and accept who you are and, more importantly, what you have become. Respect doesn't mean you agree with everything someone does or says; it means if need be, you agree to disagree. ***"Respect cannot be bought with money, it is paid for with strong character and positive self-esteem."*** Respect comes at the high price of doing the work. To get something out, you must first put something in.

Responsibility.

You must take responsibility for your actions. It doesn't matter if you are right, wrong, or indifferent, hold yourself accountable for your actions. You, alone, are in charge of what you get from life. ***"Responsibility is understanding that with choices, come consequences. Regardless of the consequences, you stand in the fire until you can walk out."*** I learned early that excuses weren't going to cut it. No matter how good the excuse, the problem still wasn't solved. George Washington Carver said, "Ninety-nine percent of all people who fail, fail because they make excuses."

My grandfather instilled in me a positive self-image, positive attitude, and the will to apply daily maximum effort to achieve my goals. I was constantly reminded that attitude and behavior were the two things I could and should control. When I woke each morning, I had the power to decide how my day would go. With positive attitude and behavior, the sky was the limit. My only bounds were those I chose to place upon myself.

I was fortunate to have such a powerful role model in my life. My grandfather helped me to understand the importance of the man in the mirror. He often said, ***"The reflection in the mirror is responsible for all of your successes and failures. There isn't ime for excuses and pointing fingers at others. There's only time to make yourself better by planning, staying positive, and, above all, doing the work. All successful people have one thing in common – they succeed because they work toward their dreams."***

> *"The reflection in the mirror is responsible for all of your successes and failures..."*

> *"All successful people have one thing in common – they succeed because they work toward their dreams."*

Through my grandfather's stories, I learned many things contributing to the successes in my life. I believe our past is a window into our future. Though I am the first to say "don't live in the past," I do recognize the need to take an occasional glance every now and then to learn from a past-life lesson. As I continue to move forward, I hear my grandfather saying, ***"Son, it's your attitude and behavior that will determine your outcome."***

As of September 17, 1997, my grandfather is looking down upon me from heaven's window. He is gone, but certainly not forgotten. I know his legacy lives on because it lives within me. It is my responsibility to continue his bequest – loving life and helping others.

My second love, track and field, took me places I never dared dream of going. Never, in my wildest imagination, could I have anticipated running would take me on a fantastic journey around the world and within myself. I competed on my high school track team, where running was just something to do. It kept me in shape for my primary sports, basketball and football. Many times I finished first in track, but I was not passionate about the sport and did not recognize my sprinting abilities. I had an incredible high school track coach, Claude Simmons, who, like my grandfather, could bring out the best in me. He was a great motivator and I say thanks to him for pushing me along and instilling positive energy. As I look back, I assumed everyone excelled at running. It's amazing how we often overlook our gifts. We spend a lifetime asking for more of something, not sure what, yet never realizing we already have everything we need. It's the "can't see the forest for the trees" syndrome.

It's amazing how we often overlook our gifts. We spend a lifetime asking for more of something, not sure what, yet never realizing we already have everything we need.

Although I attended college on both track and academic scholarships, my passion for running was nonexistent. Even though I excelled at the college level, I did not appreciate my abilities. Because of the values instilled in me – honoring your commitments, being dedicated, and staying the course, I attended practice and worked hard every day to be successful. But my heart was not in it. As far as I was concerned, when my college career was over, I would never compete in track again. That was just the beginning of the fantastic journey to discovering the true meaning of ***Focus on the Final Seconds***!™

The 1988 Summer Olympics brought me a renewed interest in track. Although I was interested again, I stayed away from it for six years before I stopped saying "what if?" and started to train again. This time, I had a different feeling – a passion and a hunger to be the best I could be. I was training and running for the most important reason of all – I wanted to! For the first time in my life, I realized my dreams were an inside job. Everything I wanted, needed, and desired started on the inside of Almon.

Finally, I had a sense of direction.

As a result of hard work and several coaches who believed in me (Larry Monts, Bob Symmons, John Long, Jodie Hale, Mike Long and Andrea Bowman), I qualified for the 1992 and 1996 Olympic Trials. I was forced to look at myself and decide what I was willing to give up to do my best. Nothing could compare to the feeling of representing the United States in international competition. All of my hard work and sacrifices were well worth it. I experienced, firsthand, the success from positive effort and sacrifice. I was responsible for my happiness, attitude, behavior, successes, and failures in the game of life.

...I was forced to look at myself and decide what I was willing to give up to do my best.

Track took me to fourteen countries where I experienced many cultures and saw things I had only read about. It gave me the opportunity to free my mind and be open to life's many possibilities. It provided the reality that practice was just that, practice and nothing more. It was a team sport dependent upon each individual's effort on meet day. My effort and hard work could and would determine the success of the team. My success on and off the track required maximum daily effort. If I were going to be successful in life, I would have to practice like I planned to play.

So through my grandfather and track I learned to play the hand I was dealt. No complaints, no excuses, and definitely no whining. To win at life, you gotta wanna! No one can wanna for you. The game of life is yours to win or lose.

An Encouraging Word

There is a time when everyone comes to a crossroads in life. It requires reflection about where you have been, where you are now, and, most importantly, where you are going. You review your options (or lack thereof), decisions (right or wrong), and opportunities for improvement and success.

Focus on the Final Seconds!™ Is about being the best you can be every day – so you will never have to say "what if?" or "I wish I would have ..." The book focuses on maximizing your effort daily and taking the steps required to achieve your success. I hope the following pages will help you find the desire, dedication, and determination to achieve your Maximum Velocity Performance. (desire and dedication plus determination)^2 equals Maximum Velocity Performance. We can all be MVPs in the most important game of all – life!

Inner Strength

No doubt, there is something to be said for being happy and having everything go right. We are encouraged to revel in the good times. But what about those less than happy, not so good days? Those periods where nothing goes your way and no one is on your side? Believe it or not, the tough times should be most revered.

Adversity and challenges help us to build strength. Adversity creates challenge, and challenge creates change. If there is no change and challenge, there can be no growth. In other words, we need the bad and adverse to appreciate the good. We need the lows in order to appreciate the highs, the pain to appreciate the laughter in our lives.

The down days are necessary to help us grow, but they don't last forever. We hang on until we make the breakthrough to achieve happier days.

Don't wait for someone else to start the fun; become your own catalyst. Remember, change and challenge are necessary for growth. Push beyond your limits, because your limits are not meant to confine you, but to challenge you by raising the bar.

So read this book with an open mind, with a can-do, positive attitude. Imagine the possibilities you face daily and identify the opportunities every day. ***"If a person wants to change his position in life, he must first change his mind."***

Adversity and challenges help us to build strength. Adversity creates challenge, and challenge creates change. If there is no change and challenge, there can be no growth. In other words, we need the bad and adverse to appreciate the good. We need the lows in order to appreciate the highs, the pain to appreciate the laughter in our lives.

The down days are necessary to help us grow, but they don't last forever. We hang on until we make the breakthrough to achieve happier days.

Don't wait for someone else to start the fun; become your own catalyst. Remember, change and challenge are necessary for growth. Push beyond your limits, because your limits are not meant to confine you, but to challenge you by raising the bar.

So read this book with an open mind, with a can-do, positive attitude. Imagine the possibilities you face daily and identify the opportunities every day. "If a person wants to change his position in life, he must first change his mind."

CHAPTER ONE:

The Winning Formula

CHAPTER ONE:
The Winning Formula

Focus on the Final Seconds!™ is driven by a formula that assures success when you properly execute it. The formula is designed to provide a solid foundation and structure leading to daily consistency. Consistency is the component separating the good from the great, the contender from the champion, and the player from the legend. Successful people consistently do things right. Sure, they make mistakes, but they make fewer mistakes than others. Champions identify a process for success and then stick to it.

***Focus on the Final Seconds!*™ winning formula consists of the following components: desire, dedication, and determination squared, equaling Maximum Velocity Performance.** You may ask yourself, "Why is the equation squared?" To fully achieve your Maximum Velocity Performance, you must make the connection between your mental and physical self. Mental and physical fitness go hand in hand: sharp body, sharp mind. As you continue your journey through this book, you will discover how your mind and body work together to help you achieve.

Just knowing the winning formula is not enough. You must implement each component to reach your maximum potential. You must implement, apply yourself, execute, and work smart. No matter how well thought out the plan, it isn't good if you don't work it.

> *The one thing all successful people do well is work at being successful.*

The one thing all successful people do well is work at being successful. Each day they risk the possibility of failure, so they may succeed. It takes courage to be brave when the outcome is not certain. Courage is centered on your faith in yourself and in others. Remember, the only bad risk you will ever take is to risk nothing at all.

To reach your goals and make your dreams a reality, you must start at the beginning. What is the beginning? The nearest mirror is a great place to start. Your first task is to take a mental and physical inventory of yourself at this moment. Take a personal assessment of your dreams, goals, accomplishments, and opportunities for improvement. Remember, it's not where you start in life, it's where you finish. Your checkup is the key to becoming an MVP in the game of life.

The following questions are designed to help you establish your starting point. Provide an answer to each question. Then review each answer and determine why it is or is not what you want it to be. The summary you provide for each question is the initial step to recognizing your strengths and opportunities for improvements. Be honest with yourself when answering these questions. After all, this is your personal assessment and only you will know how you answered. Or as my grandfather would say: ***"When you catch a fish and release it, the fish knows you caught him and you know you caught him. That's all that really matters."*** No matter how you answer, the mirror doesn't lie. You can fool a lot of people, but when you look in the mirror, you can't fool yourself.

The following questions are a guide to assess yourself mentally and physically.

1. Do you get a mental workout daily from work, books, or other sources? Please explain.

____
____
____
____
____
____
____
____

2. Are you satisfied with your current physical condition? Why or why not?

____
____
____
____
____
____
____
____

3. Do you allow yourself quiet time or take the opportunity to meditate daily? Please describe.

4. Do you have specific physical fitness goals? If so, list them.

5. Is your current fitness program providing the results you want? Why or why not?

6. Do you consider your current fitness program (mental and physical) a routine or ritual? (Do you do it just because you know you should or is it a lifestyle?) Please give some of your thoughts.

7. Does your diet complement and enhance your fitness programs and goals? Please explain.

8. When you work out, do you feel better mentally as well as physically? Please give some of your thoughts.

9. Are your career goals aligned with your personal goals? Please elaborate.

10. Are you training mentally and physically every day to achieve your goals? Please explain.

Now that you have taken your self-checkup, let me be the first to congratulate you. You have identified your starting point mentally and physically. So how did you do? Did some of your answers surprise you? Did you do better than you thought you would?

By completing the self-checkup you can identify your options. What are your options for soaring to new heights and making the quantum leap? Options are valuable when developing your strategy for success, because they allow you more than one path to achieve your goals. It is important to know and plan your options carefully so you can deal with minor setbacks or mishaps. When striving to become an MVP, proper preparation allows for greater flexibility. Options allow for patience, endurance, and adaptability. Take a moment to review and write down your options.

You'll believe it when you see it, so write it down.

____
____
____
____
____
____
____
____

Without knowing your options, it's hard to achieve your goals. Think of it this way: how are you going to win the game if you don't know why you are playing?. If you aimlessly take a shot in the dark, you are bound to miss more than you hit. Sure, there are some days you will hit the target, but more days than not you will miss your mark, or even worse you'll hit something you shouldn't have. Don't leave your success to chance. Prepare to win by identifying, evaluating, and prioritizing your options for success.

After weighing your options it is time to strategize and look at the big picture. I know what you're thinking: "you mean I have to plan and organize?" You certainly do. I never said this was going to be easy. Success comes with a big price tag called work. Better yet, it's called hard work. This is where the walk gets separated from the talk. My grandfather said, ***"Put up, suck it up, get up, or shut up."*** The world is full of big talkers and little walkers. You don't have to make noise to get it done. Everyone knows thunder makes the noise, but it's lightning that does the work.

The following is a process that works when it comes to seeing the big picture and achieving your goals. I refer to this process as the ***Focus on the Final Seconds!***™ **Summit Cycle.** This is a seven-step process to assure you will land high when shooting for the stars.

Seven Step Summit Cycle

1. **Dream** – Everything begins in the heart and mind. Each great achievement began in the mind of one person. That individual dared to dream and believe it was possible to achieve. Take some time to allow yourself to ask, "What if?" Think big. Dream of the possibilities for yourself, your family, and for others. Don't allow yourself to be negative and – more importantly – don't let the negative thinking of others penetrate your dream. Self-image is the key. Life is too short to let it go. Remember, your success is an inside job. You possess all the tools needed on the inside to reach the Summit. Discipline creates consistency and hope keeps everything alive. Hold on to your dreams, for you never know which one will make you complete.

2. **Believe** – Your dreams need to be big - something beyond your capabilities, but believable. You must believe, if things happen at the right time, if others help, if you work hard enough, it can be done. You must believe in the possibility of making the quantum leap and going to the next level. Your dreams should not be considered a fairytale – they must be attainable and real. Be confident and believe in your ability to succeed. Above all, trust your decisions. If you are to win, you must first believe you will.

3. **See** – Great achievers have the extraordinary ability to see things. They are visionaries. Long before they have the multimillion-dollar complex, they see it. They envision crossing the finish line first. The great ones saw themselves as great, long before we ever knew of them. Jordan rehearsed the big shot millions of times in his head. Bill Gates knew Microsoft would be a computer giant. World-class speakers pictured themselves speaking with energy and emotion. You must see yourself winning before the game is ever played. All of these things groom the mind to control the body, to carry out the dream. For example, I was CEO of my company at age thirteen. I used to walk around my back yard pretending to be in charge of my company. I could see the building, clients, and employees.

4. **Tell** – One reason many dreams never go anywhere is because the dreamer keeps it all to him/herself. It is a quiet dream, alive only inside his/her mind. They hold on tight to the dream without sharing it with others. You must tell your dream to many people. As you continually say it, you begin to believe it more and more. It becomes a ritual versus a routine. Daily, you know your goal and it

becomes a lifestyle. Also, it holds you accountable. When you tell others, it spurs you on to do the work. Telling others allows you to develop allies – individuals who are as dedicated to being successful as you are. Sharing your dreams with others is one way to identify your true friends. True friends encourage, empower, embrace, and enlighten.

5. **Plan** – Every dream must take the form of a plan. The saying, "you get what you plan for," is true. Your dream won't just happen. You need to sit down and plan out your strategy on a regular basis. Think through all the details. Break down the plan into small, workable parts. Then set a time frame for accomplishing each task. Proper planning allows for greater flexibility and adaptability. Planning allows you to overcome mishaps and obstacles. The better prepared, the more flexible you can be. Plot your course to eliminate re-work or downtime. Proper planning on the front end engenders efficiency and smooth execution on the back end.

6. **Work** – Wouldn't life be great if we could quit before this step? This step is where the rubber meets the road. It requires effort on your part. Unfortunately (or fortunately), successful people are usually the hardest working. While the rest of the world watches reruns, achievers work toward their goals and dreams. Consider this equation: your short-term tasks, multiplied by time, equal your long-term accomplishments. If you are consistent in your short-term tasks for a substantial period of time, you will achieve your long-term goals. The little wins eventually add up to achieve one big goal. If you work on your goals each day, you will achieve your dreams. Achieving your dreams requires maximum effort daily. The great ones consistently do things right. They work at getting it right all day, every day.

7. **Enjoy** – When you have reached your goals and you are living your dreams, enjoy your success. You achieved it the old-fashioned way, you earned it. In fact, enjoy the trip too. Give yourself some rewards along the way and an even bigger reward when you get there. Help others enjoy it. Be gracious and generous. Use your dreams to better others. Have you noticed how successful people are the ones who give the most back to others? There's that word again: consistent. Be a source of inspiration for your family and friends. Then go back to step one and dream a little bigger next time!

I hope these seven steps help you put your plan in motion. Whatever your plan for success, it only has a chance if you work it. Trust yourself to win. So many times we plan, but we don't fully trust our decisions or we lose confidence in our abilities to succeed. Don't bail out or abandon your plan at the first sign of trouble. Stay the course and trust yourself to win.

Realize, when you become clear on where you are going, the adversity starts. At times, the more positive you are, the more negative the world seems. It is important to realize that not everyone will be cheering you on. In fact, there will be many who want to see you fall short of your goals. We seem to crave the negative more than the positive, more bad than good. We would rather be spectators than participants.

Life isn't a spectator's sport. If you choose to sit and watch, it passes you by. To get the best out of life you must participate. Your success hinges on your ability to have a positive attitude and behavior. Associate with individuals who are positive and who are playing to win like you. Look for individuals who know it isn't where you start, but where you finish that counts. Gravitate toward those who cheer you on and motivate you to never give up on your dreams. Make the decision to win and stay the course. Positive attitude and behavior will drive out negativity every time. You won't have to walk away from negative people, because they will select themselves out. Your positive energy and the positive energy of others will keep them at bay.

Map your plan for success and go get it. Spend your energy on being kind, good, and right and the rest will take care of itself. Don't let others get you off track. Your success is your responsibility, and once you have your process for success in place, execute it. Evaluate your progress and make adjustments when needed, but trust the process you have selected. Don't let the talk of others affect the way you walk. Your true essence is measured by your walk, not your talk.

Your winning formula will always be based on your level of desire, dedication, and determination. How much do you desire to be the best you can be? What level of dedication is within you to make it happen? How determined are you to see it through to the end? These are the things you must ask yourself, things only you can answer. When you answer these questions positively with 100 percent commitment, you will be well on your way to achieving your MVP (Maximum Velocity Performance) in the game of life.

Notes

CHAPTER TWO:

Mental and Physical Fitness: Connect the Dots

CHAPTER TWO:
Mental and Physical Fitness: Connect the Dots

Fitness: put into a suitable state; made ready. Sound physically and mentally.

Mental: relating to the mind or to the intellectual as contrasted with emotional activity.

Physical: having material existence; relating to material things.

Mental and physical fitness combines your emotional intellect with your physical self. It's the connection between a positive state of mind and your desired physical existence.

Your mind is your most powerful attribute. It can be conditioned and trained such that **if you believe, you can achieve.** When you put positive thoughts in, you get positive thoughts and actions out. To explore just how powerful our thoughts are, take a moment to participate in the following mental exercise. Think of one of your most successful moments or one of the happiest moments in your life. Now, hold that image in your head and ask yourself the following questions:

What is your state of mind?

____

____

How is your energy?

____

____

How do you feel physically?

____

____

____

Are you excited?

___

___

___

Do you want to share your experience with others?

___

___

___

Engaging in that exercise, most likely you felt mentally and physically great. You had a positive state of mind and were full of energy, probably enough energy to light up Las Vegas. Physically you felt charged and excited and you may have had a smile on your face. Right?

Let's try one more exercise, to make sure you are making the connection. Think of a personal physical accomplishment you are proud of and ask yourself the same five questions. The physical accomplishment could be something as simple as completing a walk around the block or as extraordinary as completing a marathon. Did you find that no matter the accomplishment, mental and/or physical, your mind and body were doing and saying the same things? Did you find that "positive-in" produced "positive-out?" Most likely, your answer is yes! From the above exercises you can see there is a definite connection between your mental and physical state.

From these exercises we clearly see that if we keep our thoughts and actions positive, mentally and physically we feel better about who we are. Our self-image improves tremendously. So why do we spend so much time getting angry and upset about things we cannot control?

When I used to get angry, I felt I was in control of the situation. Looking back, I realize I was wrong. It took me a while to figure out what my grandfather meant when he said, ***"When you get mad, all you get is mad."*** The situation remains the same. The problem still exists and there is no solution. You give energy to the problem instead of the solution.

"When you get mad, all you get is mad."

Worst of all, when you are mad at someone, the person either doesn't know it, forgets it, or doesn't care. So you are left to argue with yourself. Mad really stands for **Make A Decision.** You make the decision to see the glass as half-full or half-empty. The decision to be positive or negative regarding any situation is up to you. So the next time you find yourself being mad, make a decision.

Change and adversity are parts of living, but our attitudes and behaviors determine whether we clear the hurdle or crash into it.

Part of becoming an MVP in the game of life is recognizing the role your mind and body play in predicting the outcome of your situation. Remember, growth comes only through challenge and change. Change is the one constant we can count on in our lives. Change should be embraced instead of frowned upon. Change and adversity are parts of living, but our attitudes and behaviors determine whether we clear the hurdle or crash into it. No matter how hard we fight it, resist it, or dislike it, change will happen. To cope with change, we must realize that our attitude and behavior toward change make the difference between existing and living. Through adversity, leaders are born and through positive thoughts come positive actions. Make the connection mentally and physically by controlling the two things in life you can – attitude and behavior.

Attitude and Behavior

By Almon Gunter

There are two things in life you control,
Or at least that's what I was told.
My grandfather said there're only two flavors,
When it comes to attitude and behavior.
Good and bad are the two,
What you do with them is up to you.
Choose bad you've lost before you've begun,
Choose good and you'll hit a homerun.
Attitude and behavior are where it begins,
So control them wisely so you can win.

Be a catalyst for getting results by preparing for mental and physical longevity. Feed your mind and body daily. Your body is the temple housing your most valuable asset, your mind. Mental fitness allows you to overcome distractions so you keep on track.

You're probably thinking: "How am I supposed to find the time to feed my mind and body? There are not enough hours in the day to get it all done." But you can create more time by practicing time management.

Our world seems to be in fast forward. We live in a "now" world – we need it right now and want instant gratification. Yet we are playing a game won by patience and persistence. We can't rush things. Life happens at its own pace and we all get 24 hours a day to get it all done. So it is up to each of us to utilize the time in the most efficient and productive manner. The time we don't use, we lose. Once the day is gone, it's gone and we can't get it back. If we are fortunate enough to see tomorrow, we get a fresh 24 hours to use as we see fit.

A good starting point for time management is to review your daily processes. Evaluate your day to identify tasks you can cut or perform more efficiently. It is imperative that you take care of your body and mind now, so they will take care of you later. Investing a little time daily to assure you strengthen your mind and body today will pay off big tomorrow. I call this investing – planting the seeds for a healthy mind and body today, so you can harvest them tomorrow. There are no guarantees, but at least you give yourself the best chance by putting in effort at the front end.

It is imperative that you take care of your body and mind now, so they will take care of you later.

Nurturing and training your body and mind doesn't have to be an all-day event. Even with a minimal amount of time, 15 to 30 minutes a day, you will be surprised at the payoff. Just doing 15 minutes a day is 1 hour and 45 minutes per week, 7 hours per month, 84 hours a year. It all adds up and it's a great start to improving your mental and physical self.

You can spend this time any way you choose. You can read books to inspire and elevate you or use the time to meditate and relax. Be sure when selecting your reading material to include books for fun. Listen to motivational CDs to inspire you to step outside of your comfort zone. There are hundreds if not thousands of self-help books on tape and CD. Take a walk to unwind from the hustle and bustle of your day. Spending this time daily will go a long way toward your mental and physical longevity. No matter which medium you select, I encourage you to choose one today. Start investing in yourself and your future now.

Establish specific mental goals, such as: read one book a month that focuses on your personal development. Hold yourself accountable for reaching your goals by telling a friend or family member. Form a circle of allies that are positive and moving in the same direction as you. Upward! Remember to shoot for the stars; even if you miss, you land pretty high anyway. After all, you are striving to be the best that you can be. Write down your goals and place them where you can view them daily such as on the bathroom mirror, on the refrigerator, on the dash of your car, or anywhere that will keep it fresh on your mind. Be in the game for the long haul and know what you are playing for daily. Build in checkpoints so you can evaluate your progress and make adjustments when needed. And as you reach your mental fitness goals be sure to enjoy the accomplishments and set tougher goals the next time around.

Just as you have taken time to prepare for your mental longevity, you must develop a physical fitness strategy. If you currently do not have a fitness strategy, start one today. Getting fit physically provides you more energy and an overall healthier lifestyle.

Oh boy, did I just hear you moan again? Did you just say getting in shape hurts? Well I am here to tell you that getting fit physically doesn't have to hurt. It also doesn't have to be a three-hour marathon workout in order for you to benefit. Getting fit physically only requires committing to a minimum of 30 minutes a day of doing the appropriate exercises. You should research and implement exercises designed specifically for helping you achieve your physical fitness goals. Physical exercise is about using proper physical fitness techniques, form, mental attitude, and a "just do it" philosophy. Even the best-designed workouts are void if you don't do them. In order to benefit and get the desired results, you must do the work. Your body is a temple, so it requires the proper maintenance and upkeep to withstand the test of time. Proper exercise and diet is the perfect combination for creating a healthier physical lifestyle.

Before starting any physical fitness program it is a good idea to consult with your physician. Make sure everything is in good working order before you go for it. Get a complete physical and a go-sign from you physician. Once you have the okay to work out, start with something simple, like taking a daily walk, taking a bike ride – any activity to increase your heart rate and burn calories. Remember, physical exercise does not have to hurt to be effective. Your desired results will come from one main component – determination. Make the sacrifices, do the work, enjoy the outcome.

If you are unsure where to start, hire a personal trainer to get a jump-start. With the knowledge of physical exercise, a personal trainer can customize a program, help monitor your progress, and – most importantly – keep you accountable. Your trainer will provide the extra bit of motivation you may need from time to time.

Let's face it, some of us just can't do it on our own. It's okay as long as we get the proper guidance to help us achieve.

Just as you have developed specific goals for your mental development, develop specific goals for your physical development. Set goals that make you reach and measure your progress along the way. Think long term and prepare for a happier and healthier future. Don't be discouraged if you don't see results right away. Be realistic. As a rule, it takes months to get into shape and only a week to get out of shape. Physical fitness is an every day endeavor. All too many times we start to feel better, look great, and lose weight, then we stop doing the things contributing to our success. Once you identify a plan, stick to it. Think of it in terms of owning a car. If you don't follow the maintenance plan, eventually the car will break down. The body and mind are the same way. "Just as a car is designed to be driven, the mind and body are designed to be used." "Use it or lose it" sums it up. If you let the body and mind stay in neutral, you have a good chance of going nowhere.

As you make the connection between body and mind you will notice an inner peace. You will see the world differently, because you have a new view yourself. Your light will shine brightly within and even brighter on the outside. Others will notice without you telling them.

Once you make the connection, walk the talk every day, letting your actions speak for you. You have transitioned from a routine to a lifestyle. Daily mental and physical fitness is not work, it's who you are.

Getting fit mentally and physically is about continually learning and growing. It is about not getting comfortable in the current environment, but stepping into a bigger environment to learn and grow. For example, take on a responsibility that is more than you can handle, but allows you to learn, risk, and grow.

When you are physically and mentally fit, your mind is so big, you will always have room to grow. So step out of your comfort zone, take on new challenges, and stretch yourself. Connect your mind and body today.

CHAPTER THREE:

Desire:
Lead with Your Heart

CHAPTER THREE:
Desire: Lead with Your Heart

Desire: to want something with all your heart and mind.

Desire comes from your heart, the things you want or your innermost feelings. To be your best, you must dedicate yourself to doing what you love and to focusing on tasks providing the greatest joy and self-worth. All too often, we spend a lifetime at meaningless or unrewarding work, thinking "I meant to...." Yet "meant to" signifies we didn't complete our goal and we can never win. We will always think about what might have been if we had tried a little harder or followed our heart and completed the task.

Identify what motivates and drives you to be your best. It is the first component of the winning formula. ***"When you can look in the mirror and say 'I gave all I had and there is nothing left to give,' that is your best. When you do your best, that's all you can do."*** The 100 percent effort is all anyone can give. If your dream is from the heart you will give your best and believe it is within your reach. You will do the work and leave it all on the field.

As an athlete, time and again I have seen teams and individuals soar to unbelievable heights because they believed they could. On paper they were not the best team or individual, perhaps even considered the underdog, but when it was game time they brought more heart. Their desire and will to win was greater than their competitors' and they would not be denied the victory. They wanted it more. On paper the one thing you cannot measure is a person's heart. You cannot anticipate how an individual or team will respond under pressure. Or how they will recover from a bad play or bad call. There is no way of identifying the one thing that changes the momentum and leads an individual or team to victory.

As an athlete, time and again I have seen teams and individuals soar to unbelievable heights because they believed they could.

On paper the one thing you cannot measure is a person's heart.

Your heart bursts with pride in your time of triumph, your moment of glory. It swells with joy when you achieve the unbelievable and accomplish things you never thought possible. At the same time, the heart breaks when you face bitter defeat or disappointment. It shatters at times when love is conquered and then suddenly lost.

But that's what life is all about – the peaks and valleys, the successes and failures, the loves won and lost. The goal is to minimize the valleys, disappointments, hurts, and failures – not to fall so far, so fast. How do you minimize these negative events? By taking risks. Risk to be great, to love, to win, to be the best.

Risk appearing the fool. Risk despair, failure, and suffering. Risk putting it all on the line each and every day. Realize, the greatest risk you will ever take is not to risk at all. If you risk nothing, chances are you will do nothing, and therefore you will get nothing. Success comes at the price of risks.

Realize, the greatest risk you will ever take is not to risk at all.

To fulfill your desire, you must discover your passion. Passion is the spark igniting your flame, the catalyst for taking risks and keeping your desire burning bright. Focusing on the final seconds is an inside job. Everything you want to accomplish is within you. You hold the key to creating the future you want.

Ask yourself: how much do you want it? Once you have determined your passion, it is up to you to fan the flame. You must believe it is possible to turn your desire into reality. You must see yourself finishing first, winning it all, and achieving your goals. Hold the image in your head and write down your goals. Hang an associated picture where you will see it every day. Keep your goal(s) in front of you as a daily reminder. Wanting to be successful is just the beginning of the dream. ***"How can you win the game, if you don't know what you're playing for?"*** If you don't have goals, aspirations, or dreams, you are existing instead of living. If you don't know what or where the mark is, how can you hit it? The game of life isn't a spectator's sport. Set your mark, plan your work, and work your plan. That is how you win.

You may ask, "How do I identify the one thing that drives me?" Look within for the answer, because no one knows you better than you. You control your thoughts and actions. Most importantly, you already have everything you need to succeed. Look in the mirror and make the decision to go for it. Make it today. Don't let another day go by when you are not playing to win. Don't wake up day after day wondering why you

If you think of something consistently before you go to sleep and first thing when you wake up, pay attention.

are playing. Set your sights on a goal and start working toward it. If you think of something consistently before you go to sleep and first thing when you wake up, pay attention. It could be your spark.

Discovering your passion may not be easy, but worthwhile work never is. Don't stop looking for your spark because it hasn't hit you in the face. Some of us have many interests, so narrowing it down to one or two may not be so easy. Stay the course so you can identify your goal in playing every day.

Self-image is a key element in making your dreams come true. Belief in your own abilities will go a long way in helping you discover your passion and achieve your goal. If you don't believe in your abilities to be successful, you won't hit your mark.

With each passing day, I realize more and more, the importance of the work. No matter your passion or how much your heart is into it, if you don't do the work, chances are your position will never change. Many times we find ourselves wishing for more instead of doing what is required to get more. We pray for the task to get easier, instead of praying for our skills to be equal to the task. Look at the successful people you know. Whether their success is spiritual, social, economic, mental, or physical, the one common element is: they do the work to be the best. They don't just talk about it, they do the work or they "walk about it."

You possess the power to make it happen for you. You hold the key to achieving great things in your life, but to do so requires effort.

We pray for the task to get easier, instead of praying for our skills to be equal to the task.

It requires finding your passion and then doing the right things to assure you are successful. Desire does not quit at 5:00 P.M. or when practice is over. It's something you live day after day, week after week, month after month. It is a part of your day, a part of who you are and who you are aspiring to be. When you have the heart you will do the work without being told. You will come early and stay late. True passion has no time frame, there is no finish line or taking a day off. When it's from the heart, the work, the effort, and the love are unconditional.

We all have the power to achieve success. Yet success is just a dream for so many of us because we don't discover our true potential. We pray for the wrong things and work out of necessity rather than for love. True, often we must take on things we would rather not do, but we must not let them blur the vision of our goals. Sometimes the shortest distance to success isn't a straight line. It requires bending, stretching, and a lot of patience and persistence.

So many times we don't realize our dreams because we make excuses for not doing the work. Making excuses is so much easier than putting forth 100 percent effort day after day. When you make excuses, the problem or task is still unfinished. To realize your dream you must do the work – it is the only way to complete the task and achieve your goals.

Sometimes the shortest distance to success isn't a straight line. It requires bending, stretching, and a lot of patience and persistence.

To maximize your potential in the game of life you must have desire. You must discover passion so your work is worthwhile and each day you awake with a purpose for playing the game. Life is best when you are living, not merely existing. Life is about looking in the mirror at the end of each day, knowing you gave the best you had to offer. You have no regrets, no saying "what if?", or "I meant to do more." Don't sell yourself short by not playing to win the game each and every day.

Once you discover your purpose in life, have confidence in your decision. Don't abandon your dream at the first sign of trouble or get caught up on what others say. Hang in there and weather the storm.

It's easy to play the game if you are a spectator. On Monday morning everyone knows what the quarterback should have done on Sunday. The important thing is to be a participant in the game of life. You can achieve whatever you set your mind to do. You will see your dream when you believe it. Make the best choice you can make at the time, because once it is made you are left with the consequences. So be sure you can live with the consequences of your choices. When all is said and done, the reflection in the mirror is responsible for making you happy and getting the work done.

Don't abandon your dream at the first sign of trouble or get caught up on what others say. Hang in there and weather the storm.

No matter the obstacles you face, when you live with a purpose you manage to land on your feet. Desire lends a greater sense of flexibility, because your passion is your guiding light. Each step has purpose because your heart knows what you are playing for and directs your path.

This is your dream, your vision, your goal and if others don't understand it or can't see it, that's okay. Try not to make your dreams contingent upon what others think, say, or do. Don't get caught up in the negative pool. Negative talk and behavior have no place in your plan for success. Look for positive behavior, positive people, and positive things to support your ideas and efforts. When you are clear on what it is you want out of life, the adversity starts. You discover who is your friend or foe. Stay the course and don't try to please everyone. Bill Cosby said it best: "I don't know the secret to success, but I do know that the secret to failure is trying to please everyone."

I know what it is like to search for years, high and low, for true desire, the one thing or person to make you better. Finally, I realized that I had what I was looking for the whole time. I looked within myself for the answers and found them. When I stopped praying for easy solutions and started praying for courage, patience, and wisdom, everything came together. I decided to do the work necessary to achieve my goals and not depend on others to do the work for me. Best of all, I was doing it for the most important reason – it was for me. It wasn't about making my family proud or paying college tuition. It was about running because I wanted to run.

When I stopped praying for easy solutions and started praying for courage, patience, and wisdom, everything came together.

Track provided me with my first taste of passion outside of my love of family. For years, I trained three to four hours daily, just for the opportunity to compete against the clock. You may say "I wouldn't train that hard for anything." But you would if it was your passion.

Training to run fast was the greatest feeling in the world. I did the work gladly, day in and day out, without being told. Somewhere along the way I forgot training was hard work. It was a part of who I was and made me complete as an individual.

Today I use those same disciplines to guide my personal and professional life. My work continues to be worthwhile, so the world continues to be worthwhile. Each day I wake with the same enthusiasm for motivating youth as I did for competing in track. So my work isn't work at all. It is part of who I am and I enjoy living it every day.

W. E. B. Du Bois said, "The return from your work must be the satisfaction the work brings you and the world's need of your work. With that, life is heaven, or as near heaven as you can get. With work which you despise, which bores you, and which the world does not need – this life is hell."

"With work which you despise, which bores you, and which the world does not need – this life is hell."

I hope you find your purpose in life. I pray you find the one thing that ignites you and causes you to give 100 percent effort daily. I believe we are all destined to do remarkable work while we are here on this earth. The test is finding the gift you have to offer to the world. If you look within yourself and realize success is an inside job, you will find your magic. Remember, if your heart is in it, you will surely win.

Look Within

By Almon Gunter

Where do you find the passion to live?
Where do you find the love to give?
Where do you find the power to heal?
Where do you find the strength to reveal?
Where do you find the courage to pursue?
Where do you find the strength to endure?
The answers you seek are found within,
Within you the answers begin.
The passion to live, the love to give,
The power to heal, the strength to reveal,
The strength to endure, the courage to pursue,
The answers you seek live within you!

CHAPTER FOUR:

Dedication:
Use Your Head

CHAPTER FOUR:
Dedication: Use Your Head

Dedication: committed to working hard to achieve a goal.

Dedication is the second component of the winning formula. Dedication means you are committed to making your dreams a reality. To understand dedication, you must first consider commitment. I define commitment as the decision to stay the course no matter the price. My grandfather said, ***"Commitment is when you eat bacon and eggs for breakfast and understand that the chicken participated in the breakfast because it laid the egg, but the pig was committed to the breakfast because it died in order for you to have the bacon."*** Big difference. Dedication signifies you know the price to be paid for success and you are willing to pay it.

Dedication requires using your head to stay the course. It is hard work and hard work is difficult to do day after day, week after week. Staying committed is not always easy. Life is full of obstacles to be overcome. At times, digging in and holding your ground may seem overwhelming. What should you do at such times? My grandfather often said to me, ***"Boy, work smart not hard. Use your head and think it through."***

When we allow our frustrations to get the better of us, we make our worst mistakes. ***"Out of frustration comes stupidity,"*** my grandfather said. In times of frustration, disappointment, or when things aren't going well, we make our greatest mistakes. Often we don't think things through, we get impatient, and we lose composure and self-control. We get antsy and frustrated. We forget to stay disciplined and bide the time for the right move. Our patience goes out the window and, in a blink of an eye, all our hard work goes out the door – because we didn't stay committed to the cause.

You have a better chance for success if you plan your work, then work your plan.

When you feel yourself getting offtrack, step back, reflect, and re-evaluate. Don't just react to the situation. Respond with a plan to give you the best chance of winning. I know there are times when we have to go on instinct, but don't make this your standard mode of operation.

You have a better chance for success if you plan your work, then work your plan. During your darkest hours, you can achieve your greatest accomplishments if you focus more, try your hardest, and fight with all your will to win.

Take a moment to reflect on some of your accomplishments, when you look back and wonder how in the world you ever survived. How in the midst of the storm were you able to go on?

Your answer is probably close to mine – three words: **faith** and **hard work**. You survived because your vision was clear. Your back was against the wall so everything had to come to you. You had to face your fears head-on and failure was not an option. You had faith in yourself to overcome the situation and you did the work required to overcome the obstacles.

Being dedicated requires self-motivation. Dedication is not performing a task because someone tells you to. It's not having your parents, teachers, coaches, employers, or friends stand over you to remind you of your goals. Although support is welcomed and appreciated, it's not what makes you dedicated. Dedication is when you wake up and do the work, because it's required to meet your goals. You use your head to plan your work, utilize the available resources, create opportunities where they do not exist, and, most importantly, you never give up.

Keep your head up and don't be overwhelmed or discouraged when things seem to come apart. Staying dedicated is most important. It's easy to give up when the chips are down, but during these times, the most successful people remain committed to their tasks. These times are often deemed the defining moments in a champion's life. Sunshine is great, but we need rain for the flowers to bloom at their fullest potential.

It's easy to give up when the chips are down, but...these times are often deemed the defining moments in a champion's life.

Not everyone is successful because not everyone is willing to pay the price of hard work. Not everyone is willing to stay in the game and keep fighting when they are losing by double figures and time is running out. But champions fight until the clock reads zero. They keep learning, risking, and growing. Even when the score is not on their side, they learn something of value to improve and possibly win the game next time. No matter what the day brings, keep your head in the game and stay your course.

Dedication is not just a physical component. The formula is squared for mental and physical fitness. Dedication means being a student, willing to research the work needed to achieve your goals. Know what your competition is doing and the latest resources available to you.

Sunshine is great, but we need rain for the flowers to bloom at their fullest potential.

Dedication means taking the time to learn what is best for you as well as your team. It's the ability to think things through from beginning to end. It is not always easy to keep your focus in the heat of battle, but it is during this time when your mental dedication will make the difference between success and failure. Life is filled with so many distractions and we are pulled in a million directions. But distractions and obstacles are a part of the game of life. How you choose to handle these distractions and obstacles will make the difference. The question isn't if you get knocked down, but when. Then the question isn't will you get up, but how will you get up? The greatest tool you can have in life is mental toughness.

Do you have the ability to make the right decision when the pressure is at a fever pitch? (How and why?)

____

____

____

____

____

____

Can you perform when all eyes are on you and the game is in your hands? (Why?)

____

____

____

____

____

____

Can you score the goal in the final seconds when your body wants to quit? (Why?)

____
____
____
____
____
____

Most importantly, do you want the ball in your hands when the game is on the line? (Why)

____
____
____
____
____
____

Your answers give you a good picture or your mental toughness.

How do you stay in the game? By keeping your cool. By thinking before you react. Remember, once you make a decision, you are left with the consequences of the decision. So be sure you can live with the decision and endure the outcome. Being dedicated doesn't mean you will always be right or always hit your mark, but it does mean you will always do the work needed to reach your goals. You will do what it takes to succeed and hold yourself accountable for getting the job done.

Losing your cool under pressure only adds fuel to a fire already out of control. Remember the quote from Chapter Two: ***"When you get mad, all you get is mad."*** Getting mad doesn't solve your problem; it just leaves you mad. So next time you feel you are getting mad, change it to getting MAD (Make A Decision). Focus on the answer to the situation and not the problem. After all, you know the problem, now focus on the solution.

If you maintain a level head and can think logically, you have the best chance of winning. Remember, you can't win if you are not in the game. It is hard to prevail if you mentally take yourself out of the game, so maintain your game face and never lose sight of what you are playing for. When time is running out and everyone is fatigued, your mental toughness will help you make the play that wins the game.

Legendary football coach Vince Lombardi once said, "The quality of a person's life is in direct proportion to their commitment to excellence, regardless of their chosen field of endeavor." Wherever you are in life, it is where you have chosen to be. Committing to excel isn't easy. Working day after day for a goal only you can envision requires heart and hustle. This type of dedication is rare because it demands you sometimes stand alone – just you, your goal, and the obstacles you must overcome. For you to get a lot from life, you must first give a lot.

What quality of life do you want for yourself?

Are you willing to do the work and go to battle? (Why?)

When the world is saying "you can't," will your attitude say "I can"? (Why?)

Be relentless in your effort to soar among the clouds. Look in the mirror and ask yourself: am I doing the work required to achieve my goals? (How and why?)

Are you going early and staying late if that's what's required to be successful?
(Explain.)

____
____
____
____
____
____

Do you prioritize and manage your time to overcome obstacles or do you use them as excuses to be average? (Describe.)

____
____
____
____
____
____

These are the tough questions to ask yourself. Look for the answers within you and focus on the basics. To be dedicated you don't have to be fancy, you don't have to scream or shout. To be dedicated, you simply have to do the work, day in and day out. Commit to basic things such as respect, responsibility, risk, freedom, sacrifice, preparation, and teamwork. These values shape and define who you are. They define your character and stand the test of time.

One more thing. **Don't confuse showing up every day with being dedicated.** Showing up is the first step in the dedication process, but if you do nothing when you get there, you may as well stay home and watch reruns. To be dedicated you have to show up, but once you get there you have to be there – focused on doing the work required to excel. The world won't care about what you did yesterday – it will demand the best from you each and every day. It will demand your attention and when you are not looking or lose your focus just for a second, it will kick you right in the pants. Dedication means using your head to get the most out of your body and mind to assure the work gets done day after day, week after week, and month after month. No complaints, no whining, no "what ifs?" Just good old-fashioned roll up the sleeves and do the work. That's dedication, that's using your head, that's how you win!

Dedication

By Almon Gunter

Today I decided I would start my journey,
My journey to fulfill my dreams and reach my goals.
I told myself I would start doing the work today.
I would come early and stay late if that's what it took to succeed.
As I began my first step, the way seemed to get harder,
By step two, I realized this would be no ordinary journey.
Wow, I made it through my first day, my body still intact but weary,
My mind focused, but tired.
Suddenly I realized tomorrow, yes tomorrow I get to do this all over again.
Tomorrow I get to chase my dreams and goals, yet again by working hard.
So this is what my grandfather meant when he said do the work day after day.
This is what he meant by never quit or give up.
By week two, my task grows old, but I must fight through the obstacles to keep my dreams alive.
After all the reality of my dreams are closer.
But are they really closer or is it all in my head? I guess I have to just wait and see.
I must trust the process and have faith, you know faith works not seen.
So again today, I push myself hard, only to know that tomorrow I will push myself even harder.
So day after day, week after week, month after month I will get up and do the work.
This, my friend, is dedication.

CHAPTER FIVE:

Determination: Body, Mind, and Soul

CHAPTER FIVE:
Determination: Body, Mind, and Soul

Determination: a fixed movement or tendency toward an object or end.

The third component of the winning formula is determination. Determination is your ability to explore every option available and your willingness to do the work so you can win. We are all creatures of habit and move toward the familiar things in our lives. We have a natural tendency to gravitate to what we know best and what is most comfortable to us.

Determination requires effort by any means necessary. It is not about doing what is familiar or most comfortable. It is about stepping out of your comfort zone and stretching yourself in ways you never thought possible. Determination means taking risks and challenging yourself to reach your goals. When you are determined, you know there will be change. Instead of dreading change, you embrace it, you crave it, and you thrive on it. Growth can only occur when there is change.

"What are you willing to give up to achieve your goals?"

"What are you willing to give up to achieve your goals?" my grandfather asked again and again. It seemed like no matter how I answered the question his reply was always, ***"Then what?"*** If I said I would train harder, study harder, or work smarter, he responded, ***"And then what?"*** At the time, I thought, "Good Lord, what else is there? What do you want from me?"

He wanted me to reach my full potential. He wanted me to never stop looking for ways to improve myself. To not rest on yesterday's laurels, but to use them as stepping-stones to build an even brighter future. I learned to be the student, willing to keep learning, risking, and growing. Every day I try to discover one new thing I didn't know the day before.

Every day I try to discover one new thing I didn't know the day before.

You must decide what your goals are worth to you.

How hard are you willing to work to assure you achieve your goals?
(And then what?)

____
____
____
____
____
____
____

What sacrifices will you make so you can stand on the first-place podium?
(Why?)

____
____
____
____
____
____
____

Is fulfilling your destiny worth the hard work or can you settle for goals others think you should have?
(Why?)

____
____
____
____
____
____
____

Determination is the toughest part of the winning formula. In this part of formula, if you don't dig in and do the work, it shows up in your performance. Determination exposes the big talkers and little walkers. It's easy to talk about being the best or to say you want to be number one. It's a whole different ball game when you have work to get it done.

We would all be champions if all we had to do was talk about it. We all have the ability to plan our work or plan our future, but the planning stage seems to be where most of us stop. We say we are going to get into better shape, or read more, or take more risks. Then the reality of the work sets in and we shy away from our goals. The first few weeks we may do the work, but for whatever reason, we miss a day only to say we will do it tomorrow. The next thing you know it's been a week and the work still isn't getting done. Reaching the goal starts to fade and before long we forget about the goal altogether. Then we wake up and set another goal. Well. Big news flash – no matter how many goals you set or how many times you set your goals, if you don't do the work you will not achieve them.

No matter how you look at it, achieving your goals requires you to do the work. That is why I love the sport of track and field. Track and field makes it easy to measure your success. If you come to practice every day, but choose not to focus and do the work, it shows on meet day. On the other hand, if you show up for practice every day and train to run fast, chances are you will perform well on meet day. No matter how great your coach or how much your team cheers you on, your performance is based on you getting the work done. Sounds a whole lot like the game of life, doesn't it? You get out what you put in. You know there is a name for doing the work day in and day out to achieve your goals. It's called discipline.

Discipline is defined as training to correct, mold, or perfect the mental faculties or moral character. I like to say, ***turning a routine into a ritual*** and making it a lifestyle, a part of who you are.

Let me discuss lack of discipline. I receive many requests from individuals asking for advice on how to get in shape. In many cases I help them to develop a fitness plan and say, "Okay all you have to do now is work the plan." Most of the individuals do great the first couple of weeks and I even hear from them sometimes saying how much more energized and better they feel. You would think that once an individual is getting good results, s/he would stay at it, but so many times it's not the case at all.

Usually people hit a plateau and the weight doesn't come off as fast as they want. Or they may not notice changes right away. Out of frustration, they slack off and make excuses as to why they can't continue the training program. The two excuses I hear the most are lack of time and not seeing any difference. The truth is they lack the discipline to do the work, day in and day out. Coach Vince Lombardi said, "The difference between a successful person and others is not the lack of strength, not the lack of knowledge, but rather the lack of will." The most important four-letter word in you achieving your goals is WORK. There is no way around it. I have asked hundreds of successful people their secret to success and they have the same answer, they worked at it, worked in it, and worked on it.

The most important four-letter word in you achieving your goals is WORK.

Are you willing to do the work?
(How and why?)

Do you have what it takes to reach the top?
(Why?)

Can you rebound from the occasional letdown?
(How and why?)

I know you have what it takes. You can reach the top and overcome the obstacles of life. But achieving your goals isn't based on what I believe you can do – it is based on what you believe you can do.

Determination requires self-sacrifice. You have to be willing to give of yourself even when you feel you have given it all. Determination demands you lay it on the line every day to get what you want. Lay what on the line? You must put your dreams, your hopes, and your fears right out there in plain sight every day. Take the risks and hold tightly to your dreams and never let go of them.

At times, self-sacrifice may mean you have to walk alone and remain determined to win and accept the challenge. When you think of all the things in life we enjoy – from airplanes, to computers, to cars – they came into existence because of the self-sacrifice of an individual. Someone dared to dream, dared to plan, and dared to do the work necessary to better mankind. Someone was willing to give of him/herself so we all would benefit.

Successful people give back to their family, community, and country. They understand the importance of helping others to achieve their goals. My mother often told me to have faith, hope, and charity – and of these, charity was the greatest. By doing the work and being willing to sacrifice for a greater good, you often inspire others to raise the bar and play for more in the game of life. Isn't that what it's all about? Each of us must do our part to make the world a better place.

Successful people give back to their family, community, and country. They understand the importance of helping others to achieve their goals.

When was the last time you gave of yourself to achieve your goals? I mean really left it all on the field with no regrets. In your quest to make yourself better, have you given back to help others? Determination doesn't mean stepping on others to get your way, it doesn't mean being disrespectful or being thoughtless about other's feelings. As the Nike® slogan says, Just Do It™.

I use a phrase with all of my student athletes: ***just do what I do.*** They repeat it before a test or a big game. It means don't get fancy, don't talk about it, just walk about it. Let your efforts speak for you. My track coach, Larry Monts, said, "It ain't bragging if you can do it."

"If you're gonna play the game, at least know what the rules are." We live in a "now world," where we are the microwave generation. Everything happens at lightening speed. For example, we receive astounding information in a few computer keystrokes. I see so many people trying to win the game with speed. But speed won't help you win the big game.

You need patience and persistence. Learn how to wait to excel. Plan your work and be ready when the opportunity presents itself.

Many people who say they are determined are only willing to do the work for a week or two. Nothing in life worth having comes easily or quickly. Rome wasn't built in a day, so it's safe to say you will not achieve your goals overnight. If you don't hit your mark in a day or two, it doesn't mean you won't hit your mark at all. Give yourself time.

In an interview, a newspaper reporter asked my grandfather about my success in track. He said, *"My grandson was a long shot who kept shooting."* I love that quote. We are all long shots in this game of life, but we have to keep shooting to have a chance at scoring. After all, to win the game you have to score and the only way to score, you guessed it, is to keep shooting!

"My grandson was a long shot who kept shooting."

Prepare your body and mind to endure the journey by putting good things into them. Your body is a temple and it is the only temple you get, so take care of it. Feed your mind with positive input. At all cost, stay out of the negative pool! (Even the shallow end of the negative pool.) Get in touch and stay in touch with who you are. You are your own guiding light.

That reminds me of a story my grandfather told:

> *A boy caught a firefly (lightning bug) and placed it in a jar. He was fascinated by the way the bug could light up. Being curious, the boy rushed home to ask his mother. He said, "Mom, I caught this firefly today. What makes it light up?" The mother looked at the bug and said, "I don't know. Let's ask your father when he gets home. He thinks he knows everything anyway." When the dad got home the little boy said, "Dad I caught this firefly today. What makes it light up?" The father got that "deer in the headlights" look and said, "I don't have a clue." The mother said, "Now why am I not surprised by that answer?" The boy set the jar on the table and watched the firefly light up. About 30 minutes later he ran to his parents and said, "Mom, Dad, I figured out what makes the bug light up." His parents looked at him and said, "What?" The boy said, "It's what's on the inside. That's what makes the bug light up."*

The moral of the story: what's inside determines how brightly your light will shine.

Body, Mind, and Soul

By Almon Gunter

I will train my body to endure the pain,
To help me rise when I'm knocked down again.
I will stay determined no matter the cost
If I lose my focus, my dreams are lost.
I must stay persistent and bide my time,
To win this game I must use my mind.
I must think it through the best I can,
I must plan my work and work my plan.
I will work in the morning, even all night long,
I will not stop till the game is won.
When my way gets hard, I will not fold,
I'll keep it together body, mind, and soul.

CHAPTER SIX:

Making the Quantum Leap

CHAPTER SIX:
Making the Quantum Leap

Desire, dedication, and determination are the three essential components of the winning formula. They each play a key role in helping you obtain your goals. If you take the time to develop your mind as well as your body, good things will happen. I did not say good things will happen overnight, but they will happen if you stay the course. To achieve your Maximum Velocity Performance in the game of life, you must have these three components and you must call upon each component every day.

Being successful isn't easy. It requires you to give of yourself in ways you never thought possible. But nothing worth having comes easily or without some personal sacrifice. ***"If something comes easily, you might want to consider running in the other direction."***

> ***"If something comes easily, you might want to consider running in the other direction."***

When some-one's offerings sound too good and claim to take little time and effort…watch out. Infomercials are great examples. The infomercial host makes it sound and look so easy to succeed, if you use the product. The desired results seem to magically appear in days. Realize, if it were that easy, we all be on white, sandy beaches, drinking fruity concoctions decorated with umbrellas. Don't believe the hype. To achieve and make the quantum leap, you have to roll up your sleeves and do the work.

> ***To achieve and make the quantum leap, you have to roll up your sleeves and do the work.***

A quantum leap has several definitions. ***Physics*** definition one: a transition of an atomic or molecular system from one discrete energy level to another with concomitant emission or absorption of radiation having energy equal to the difference between the two levels. Definition two: a sudden change or increase, as in knowledge or information.

Definition one is used in physics. The words transition and energy level are important. In Chapter One, we discussed how getting fit physically changes your energy level. Your body slowly makes the transition from being inactive to active and provides you with more energy. As a matter of fact, when you have a lifestyle of daily workouts and miss a single workout, you feel sluggish and drained. Your body feels cheated and your energy level seems to drop a notch or two. You feel like you have been unplugged from your energy supply.

The second part of definition one takes into account the absorption or emission of another energy source and the difference between the two energy sources. The second source of energy is the mental component.

Definition two clearly states a sudden change or increase in knowledge or information. Developing your mind is key to overcoming life's obstacles and staying the course. The mind is what gives us hope in our pursuits. Thus, the winning formula for the game of life has to be squared. Mental and physical fitness are equally important in the development of who you are. Some things in life are just meant to go together, such as: peanut butter and jelly, macaroni and cheese, or cookies and milk. Mental and physical fitness are in that same category. One without the other doesn't seem right.

Mental and physical fitness are equally important in the development of who you are.

For some of us, success seems to be just out of reach. Why? In large part, it is due to self-limitations we impose. We are our own worst critics. We impose limitations on ourselves all of the time – why we can't achieve, why it didn't work out, or what could we have done better. Hindsight is always 20/20 and rightfully so, because you are working with additional information gained through experiencing the event.

If you are going to make the quantum leap and change your position in life, the sideline isn't where you want to be.

If we remove the barriers in our minds and do the work necessary to achieve our goals, chances are we will succeed. Keep an open mind and start at ground zero – don't disqualify yourself before you play the game. Listen to all the instructions before you bail out and sit on the sideline. If you are going to make the quantum leap and change your position in life, the sideline isn't where you want to be. It's like saying you want to win the lottery, but you never buy a ticket. For a winning chance, you must buy a ticket. Life is the same way. If you are going to win, you must first get in the game. So get off the sidelines and start playing.

Once you remove your limitations you must do the work that is required to achieve your goals. There's that phrase again, "do the work." Nothing worth having will be achieved without working for it. You have to make the time to do the work, but only if your goals are important to you.

I can always tell when someone is serious about reaching his or her goals. These individuals are focused on doing the work required. Time waits for no one. You can spend your time talking about it or walking about it. If we spend as much time working toward our goals as we do convincing ourselves why we can't reach them, we would be successful more times than not.

Having the right attitude and behavior is everything. *"Attitude and behavior are the two things that you control and they only come in two flavors, good or bad."* The glass is always half-full if you choose it to be. No matter what happens, you can control your attitude and behavior throughout the day. Push beyond your limits, working diligently to make life happen the way you want. After all, it is your life.

"Attitude and behavior are the two things that you control and they only come in two flavors, good or bad."

Your limits do not exist to confine you, but to challenge you to achieve great things. Limitations help you commit to channeling your energy so you can maximize your efforts and results. When you break through the barriers, you realize the things holding you back made you stronger and more efficient. The more you expand your limitations, the more commonplace tough situations become. If you keep pushing beyond your limits and tearing down the walls, you will keep growing.

Finding the time to bring these two energy sources together (mental and physical fitness) will not be easy. You will have to stop time in order to gain more time. That means working efficiently and planning your work to be successful. Use your time and energy wisely by creating your own road map for success.

Study your plan of attack again and again. Then work your plan to its fullest potential, always remembering to control what you can. Once you start your attack, don't let up. Once you decide it is "go time" and start to execute your plan, don't worry about what to do next. Keep attacking. ***"Once you start your plan, never stop attacking."*** Work smart, work hard, and work efficiently. That is how to create more time for you to be successful.

> *"Once you start your plan, never stop attacking."*

Desire, dedication, and determination reflect your will to win. Decide for yourself what you want and then maintain that level of intensity. Be confident in your decisions and make your decisions based on what you see happening and not what others say is happening. The Greatest (Muhammad Ali) said after first winning the world heavyweight boxing championship, "I am gonna be champ the way I want to be champ, not the way you think I ought to be champ."

We need to concentrate on being the champ in our own way. You know what your dreams are, you know what your level of commitment is, you know what you are willing to sacrifice, you know how hard you are willing to work. You decide what you want for yourself.

Don't misunderstand. Getting input from others and lining up allies to help is great, but in the end it's you alone on the line to achieve your goals. The mirror won't hold Mom, Dad, sister, brother, or friends accountable for not achieving your goals. The reflection you see in the mirror is accountable each and every time. No matter how hard you try to convince yourself someone else was at fault for your not succeeding, it won't fly.

As owner of Gunter - Gunter, Inc., I thought about writing books to support my seminars and clients. For years, I wanted to provide materials to inspire others to reach their maximum potential in the game of life. I kept thinking I was not ready, I had too many things going on and didn't have the time. All the usual excuses. But I couldn't lie to the mirror. The reason I wasn't writing was because I chose not to write. I wasn't prioritizing, stopping time, or creating the opportunity to excel.

Using the experience from my track career, the tools of desire, dedication, determination, commitment, drive, and discipline, I wrote my books. Since making the decision a year ago, I have created this book, ***Focus on the Final Seconds!***™, and four playbooks on mental and physical fitness. I stopped talking about it and decided to walk about it. In addition, I have the titles and research for three other books. It is amazing what you can accomplish when you do the work. Maintain your passion and will to succeed and you will win.

Making the quantum leap demands you turn it up a notch, meaning you come early and stay late. It demands you walk the talk every day and not just when the coach or other players are watching. When you make the quantum leap, you don't have to tell anyone or toot your own horn. Everyone will know.

When you make the quantum leap, you don't have to tell anyone or toot your own horn. Everyone will know.

It's easy to identify the people in life who are playing for so much more. You can pick them out of a crowd. They have a different walk and a different style. There seems to be a glow or some type of light within and all around them. You want to go to their light – you are attracted to their energy like a moth to flame.

That is why so many people identify with sports. When you watch teams or individuals compete, there is so much passion and energy in the competition. In the stadium, you get goose bumps from the introduction of the players.

We want to be around positive people, but being positive 24/7 is easier said than done. Many are called to be positive but only a few seem chosen. The chosen few are the cream of the crop – the ones who seem to make their way out of no way at all.

Are you one of the chosen few? (How do you know you are?)

Have you turned it up a notch?
(How?)

Does the light within you burn bright enough for others to see? (How do you know?)

____
____
____
____
____
____
____
____

Do you possess the little something extra that make others want to be in your space?

____
____
____
____
____
____
____
____

I know you have it within you to make the quantum leap. We all have it. We were all created with a wonderful gift to share with the rest of the world.

Have you discovered what your gift is yet? Have you unlocked the secret within you for achieving your maximum velocity performance in the game of life? If you haven't, what are you waiting for? The clock is ticking.

Putting It All Together

By Almon Gunter

Desire, step one of the winning formula, is a matter of the heart,

The heart I am told is where all of your dreams must start.

Dedication, step two of the formula, is the ability to use your head

To achieve those things often thought of but rarely ever said.

Determination, step three of the formula, body, mind, and soul

Doing the work to win the game without ever being told.

To make the quantum leap and go where few others have gone,

Requires mental and physical fitness both equally as strong.

You must put it all together if you are to ever have a chance,

To be among the chosen few who experience a victory dance.

You must put it all together when you're knocked down and hurt,

Pick yourself up, dust yourself off, and continue to do the work.

Making the quantum leap, my friend, is never an easy task,

It requires heart, hustle, enthusiasm and a will that always lasts.

So make the decision to do the work and train no matter the weather,

For the only way you will win this game, is by putting it all together.

CHAPTER SEVEN:

Maximum Velocity Performance (MVP)

CHAPTER SEVEN:
Maximum Velocity Performance (MVP)

Now that you have the energy to make the quantum leap, you are ready to perform every day at your maximum velocity performance. You are ready to become an MVP in the game of life. When you perform at your maximum, you are performing at your best. And when you perform at your best, you eliminate the "what ifs?" and the "I shoulda, woulda, couldas" in your life. One of the most disheartening things in the world is living with the "what ifs?" every day.

Being an MVP means you will not settle for anything less than giving 100 percent effort daily. Not just giving 100 percent when everyone is watching, but giving 100 percent because of who you are and what you have on the inside. The 100-percent-individual effort transforms good individuals into great individuals. The things you do when no one is watching are what will make you great. The practice time and hard work you put in when you are all alone make you a champion. Folks like Michael Jordan, Walt Disney, Bill Gates, Oprah Winfrey, and Doug Williams put in a lot of time developing themselves when no one was watching. Their efforts behind the scenes resulted in astonishing accomplishments on the screen. Self-discipline and self-motivation are behaviors you must instill in yourself.

Have you ever noticed how most successful people only have one speed ... maximum velocity? MVPs operate at a higher level than the average person. They raise the bar constantly and love every minute of it. They practice much harder than they play, so performing in the game of life looks easy. They want the ball in the final seconds and they demand it. MVPs understand the difference between a hero and a zero is the willingness to take a risk when everything is on the line. They know in order to make the shot you have to take the shot. If you want to perform at your maximum, you must practice each day at your maximum. To play a perfect game, you must have perfect practices. Practice doesn't make perfect. Perfect practices make perfect.

MVPs understand the difference between a hero and a zero is the willingness to take a risk when everything is on the line.

Student athletes often ask me, "Coach, how can I run faster?" I reply, "To run fast you have to practice running fast. You can't train your mind or body at 70 percent daily and expect your mind and body to perform at 100 percent on your command. Not with any kind of consistency. It just doesn't work that way." MVPs go the extra mile. They put in the little bit extra every chance they get. I advise not to just train to be the best in your school, your city, or your state, but train to be the best person you can be – period. The world expects it of you and the game of life demands it from you.

The formula of desire, dedication, and determination squared, mentally and physically propels you to achieve your maximum. The formula is simple, but putting it together all day, every day isn't. It's much easier to talk about it than to walk about it. MVPs have no fear of failure. In fact, MVPs understand to be successful they will experience failure along the way. After all, what is success? Isn't it just persistence and the will to win? Sure it is! It's the long shot who keeps shooting; it's the dancer who keeps dancing. MVPs are not born, they are made. They make themselves through blood, sweat, and tears. They go out every day and put it all on the line. You never have to question their desire, dedication, or determination. They are driven to be better than the best and they have the discipline, self-motivation, and self-determination to get the job done.

The formula of desire, dedication, and determination squared, mentally and physically propels you to achieve your maximum.

The winning formula is not a magic formula. There is no trickery or sleight of hand in its power to help you achieve. You could not buy the winning formula with all the money in the world, because money isn't the currency it respects. Even if you could purchase the formula, it wouldn't do any good unless you did the work. Work makes this formula unique.

I have provided the pillars or principles on which the formula is built. The pillars of desire, dedication, and determination wrapped tightly in mental and physical fitness. Each working independently and with the others to develop you into an MVP. You can't buy desire, dedication, or determination; you can't wish it into you. You must instill them to have the ingredients for a healthier and happier lifestyle.

Your finest hour will come when your back is against the wall and you stare at adversity and believe you will win.

Your maximum, your best, day after day will come when you have trained your body, mind, and soul. Your finest hour will come when your back is against the wall and you stare at adversity and believe you will win. You will win when you commit 100 percent. No holding back, no whining, no wishing for an easier way. Your day will come when you look in the mirror and decide you want to be the best and you are willing to do the work necessary to achieve your goals.

MVPs are not a dime a dozen. They are an elite group of individuals who have raised the bar for their personal and professional lives.

MVPs are not a dime a dozen. They are an elite group of individuals who have raised the bar for their personal and professional lives. MVPs do not conform to what others think, they don't fall prey to what others say. They don't hide in the shadows of life. MVPs are out front for the whole world to see, working quietly and diligently day in and day out.

You are an MVP in the game of life. I know you have what it takes to get to the top. You are a leader and your own catalyst, empowering, enlightening, encouraging, and embracing life, so you can help others do the same. You are not on the bench watching the game of life; you are not a spectator. You are a participant.

You are ready to take on the competition in the biggest game of all – the game of life. This is what I think of you, but what's important is what you think of you. Your opinion matters most. When you look in the mirror do you see success? Do you see a person with a:

Sense of Direction
Understanding of the Game
Commitment to Be the Best
Courage to Stand Alone
Education on What It Takes to Win
Superior Attitude
Superior State of Mind

I hope you do.

The greatest thing is that every day you have an opportunity to create the life you want. If you are not satisfied with where you are or with what you have achieved, you can do the work necessary to change it. You hold the key and possess the power to change your world. All you need is to just do it! Dream, believe, see, tell, plan, work, and enjoy your life. You owe it to yourself, your family, and the world. Leave a legacy that shows your desire, dedication, and determination to be the very best. A legacy that shows you didn't merely exist, you lived every day to the fullest. Show you possessed and demonstrated faith, hope, and charity and of these three things charity was your greatest gift to the world.

You hold the key and possess the power to change your world.

If we are to have a caring world, a world of peace and prosperity, it is up to each of us to do our part in creating such a world. The universe needs you to be turned on and fired up about living – not just existing. It needs you to lead from the front and to be a big walker, not a big talker. Together, we can become MVPs in the game of life and win!

Notes

SUMMARY

Summary

The winning formula in the game of life is three words: desire, dedication, and determination. We understand the meanings of these words and their powers, individually and together. But making the connection mentally and physically isn't easy.

To achieve your goals you must build a foundation grounded in the principles of desire, dedication, and determination. Connecting your desired mental state with your physical self is a constant process. Doing the work and persisting through the daily boredom isn't easy.

Look within yourself and dare to dream the impossible – that is where it all begins.

Look within yourself and dare to dream the impossible – that is where it all begins. Desire means you are willing to put your heart into it. In discovering your passion, you find the will do the work. Desire means you risk something to get something. It signifies you are not a stranger to sacrifice or to making the tough decisions. You answer the bell round after round. You assess your situation, plan your work, and are willing to work the plan. Your goals are a part of you. You have adopted a lifestyle, walking the talk to become an MVP in the game of life.

Dedication requires you to become a thinker, not a feeler.

Dedication requires you to become a thinker, not a feeler. Your head is in it, so you can win. You do the work not because someone is watching or telling you, but because it is required to achieve your goals. You achieve to the best of your abilities every day. You take on all challenges, knowing there can be no growth without change. In your darkest hours, you prevail because failing is not an option. You dig in to do the work and never stop believing in your ability. Staying cool when the world around you is at a fever pitch is an art form. You practice like you want to play, so every day you push beyond your limits. The difficult becomes commonplace for you. You go beyond your limits, knowing boundaries are not confining, but challenging. You learn, risk, and grow even more.

You are bound and determined to succeed in the game of life. You are a participant, off the bench and in the game. Determination drives the winning formula because determination is the work. It means, "I will train to be great and will come early and stay late if that is what it takes." Your drive and discipline show in everything you do.

Determination signifies you are willing to do this and give this to be the best. Not the best in the city, state, or country, but to be the best – period. You compete against yourself, to improve and offer the best chance of succeeding. Thus, you inspire everyone you meet.

Becoming an MVP is no easy task. You have to give a lot to get a lot. MVPs are made, not born. They develop because of desire, dedication, and determination. MVPs are driven and disciplined and thrive on hard work and challenge. At times, the road to the top is long and lonely. Ask any winner, was it worth it? The answer 99 out of 100 times is Yes!

Becoming an MVP is no easy task. You have to give a lot to get a lot. MVPs are made, not born.

You are responsible for your life. I encourage you to discover what you are playing for and pursue it with everything you have. Find your passion and get excited about living. I encourage you to continue to learn, risk, and grow and to challenge yourself to be better. Step out of your comfort zone and go beyond your limits. I hope you will find the desire, dedication, and determination to become a success story in your own right. Then become a positive example so future generations may learn from your success. I challenge you to make the connection between the mental and physical realms. Develop a sharp body and mind to take care of you and others down the road. Achieve your Maximum Velocity Performance in the game of life. Become a champion for all ages. Leave your mark on the world in a positive way; I know you can.

They Said …

By Almon Gunter

They said I wasn't fast enough,
But yet they can't catch me.
They said I wasn't quick enough,
But they blink and I am gone.
They said I wasn't strong enough,
But I carry the team.
They said I couldn't jump high enough,
But I clear buildings in a single bound.
They said I lacked the power,
But no field, arena, or park can contain me.
They underestimated me.
That was their first mistake.
They said I would never be anything,
But I am the MVP in the biggest game of all: life
They said on paper I didn't add up.
I said of course not.
I am not a mathematical equation.
I am the reason you play the game!
I am a CHAMPION! I said …

If you have gotten only one thing out of ***Focus on the Final Seconds!***™, I hope it is the realization that, inside, you possess everything you need to be great. It's not about what they said. In the end, it's about what you said. We each have a wonderful gift to share, but we must discover it, develop it, and share it with the rest of the world. Remember to dream, believe, see, tell, plan, work, and enjoy life every day! ***Focus on the Final Seconds!*** so you can win the game of life. Once the final seconds are gone, you are left with the consequences!

Is becoming an MVP within your reach?
(Why do you think so and how do you demonstrate it?)

____

____

____

____

____

____

____

Do you have the desire, dedication, and determination to make the quantum leap and win the game of life?
(Why do you think so and how do you demonstrate it?)

____
____
____
____
____
____
____

Will you do the work mentally and physically each day to be the best?
(Why do you think so and how will you demonstrate it?)

____
____
____
____
____
____
____

THE REST OF THE STORY

THE REST OF THE STORY

Wilson Gunter

Throughout this book, you have read the words of wisdom passed on to me by my grandfather, Wilson Gunter. He had a profound affect in shaping my life and I am sure his words hit home with you as well. Perhaps you are curious as to who he was and how he influenced so many people.

Wilson Gunter was born September 11, 1906 in Maxville, Florida to Julia Wilson and Dan Gunter. One of three children, he was no stranger to hard work and hard times. He developed his strong character and work ethic from his mother and his grandfather, James Wilson.

To shed light on my grandfather's true essence, I solicited the help of several family members. My grandmother, young at 93 years of age, is the queen who knew him best. She and my grandfather met and married in 1936. As she put it, "I worked at the Mt. Brooks, Florida mill and when it relocated to Baldwin, I had the good fortune of meeting your grandfather. I still remember what he was wearing the day we met. He had on white pants and shirt and his shoes were polished. He was always a sharp dresser."

My grandfather was a stickler for having polished shoes. He used to say to me, "You can tell a lot about a man by the way his shoes look."

My grandparents had nine kids. Although my grandmother never worked in the traditional sense, she managed nine kids, qualifying as two full-time jobs. My grandfather believed his primary responsibility was providing for his family. He never felt anyone should or would give him anything. His attitude spoke volumes, "It's up to me to get it done for my family."

My grandmother commented, "He was never satisfied when it came to being a good provider. He always looked for ways to bring in just a little bit more for the family. Often after working on the railroad all day, he'd do odd jobs to bring in additional income."

My grandparents on their 50th Wedding Anniversary

As she talked about his work ethic, I couldn't help but see how he walked his talk. They had a true partnership in every sense – she trusted him to provide what the family needed and he trusted her to manage it.

My grandmother explained, "In raising nine kids, there were bound to be some discipline issues. He approached discipline as he did many things in his life –in a clear and concise manner. For the most part, he rarely had to discipline. The majority of the time, it was left up to me. The kids knew how far to go and didn't want to wake the little giant."

My grandfather was a master, who disciplined through verbal communication, never in a demeaning or harsh way, but in a way you understood. He used stories and analogies to hit his point home.

My grandmother said, "His driving force was taking care of his family. He was a firm believer in doing his best for his family and helping others. He wanted to see others prosper and prevail and he pitched in to lend a hand whenever he could. He thought a strong community could only be created through strong people who believed in each other and helped each other. He felt everyone was more alike than different, trying to make a good life from whatever they had."

My grandfather had no time for excuses. He was honest and worked hard for the good of his family and for the good of humankind.

It is said that beside every great man is a great woman. That was certainly true in my grandparents' case. They were married for 61 years.

My grandmother concluded by saying to me, "It's amazing what taking it one day at time can do for you."

Aunt Catherine Powell, the eldest daughter, described her father. "He's the strongest man I ever knew. It didn't matter the situation, work, family, or play. He always held his ground and represented himself and his family with the utmost honor and respect."

Hearing this, I imagined a lion, a symbol of pride, courage, freedom, and family.

Aunt Catherine pointed out my grandfather's ability to discipline through humor and to encourage independent thinking. "We got most of our humor from Daddy. One of the things I admired most was his ability to empower and let go. All the kids had a chance to take risks and be independent. We weren't afraid to try things or to fail."

Listening to this, I understood why my parents, especially my father, allowed me to spread my wings and fly at an early age. Independence, as I have come to understand it, has always been a Gunter trait. It has been nurtured, encouraged, and instilled in each family member.

In conversing with Aunt Catherine, I realized my grandfather's advice about being 150% everyday wasn't just something he told me. He gave 150% throughout his life. He wanted everyone, especially his family, to be the best at whatever they decided to do. My grandfather's philosophy was, ***"If you always do your best, you may not win every game, but you will learn from the experience and give yourself the opportunity to win future games."*** When it came to trust, he believed you should trust yourself first to get what you need by doing the right thing. He encouraged us to use the gift of self-discipline and the power of self-confidence to overcome any obstacles.

Aunt Catherine recalled, "No matter the choices I made in my life, good or bad, Daddy never stood in judgment. He was always there for me. He believed in treating people as individuals and was never quick to jump to conclusions. He was a great thinker and stressed the importance of 'getting it in your head.'"

My grandfather could think his way out of anything. He was patient and persistent – two characteristics that add up to success.

Aunt Hazel Gunter fondest memory of her father was his devotion to his community. She recounted, "Daddy was always willing to serve others in any way he could. He even put together a community baseball team. Baseball was his sport of choice."

He loved those Atlanta Braves. During a Braves game, he was glued to the television and everyone had to sit quietly. He used baseball to teach kids about the game of life. Maybe that's where I learned to use athletics as a vessel to get the things I wanted. I learned so many life lessons when I competed in athletics. When I was the batboy for those teams he put together, I felt I was part of something special.

Aunt Hazel added, "Daddy gave us everything we needed and most of the things we wanted. There were many times we had no clue how hard it was for him to do so."

A characteristic of an outstanding leader is that of service. Great leaders are willing to give back and serve others. Quick to help people, my grandfather did not hesitate when it came to making his community better. Best of all, he demonstrated service by his actions.

Aunt Hazel concluded, "Daddy was a symbol of strength and love."

With each story, I realized how special my grandfather was.

Uncle Lawrence Gunter, the baby boy of the group, said, "I can't put my finger on it, but he was always striving to achieve more – not for himself, but for the family. He was centered on creating a better life for us. He was a worker and a doer. He didn't just talk about it; he went out and made it happen. Daddy was like a squirrel – always working, storing, and preparing because winter was coming."

I have constantly told Uncle Lawrence he works too much, but he said, "I do so because, just as Daddy said, 'No one ever gives you anything. In life you seldom get what you deserve; you get what you work for.'"

Uncle Lawrence commented, "Daddy was a rich man – not in money and material wealth, but in the character he possessed. He was okay with whatever you wanted to do or become in life. But you had to be honest, straightforward and do your best. He gave each of us the opportunity to be whatever we wanted to be. We were rich in so many ways. Rich in family, love, kindness, and being there for each other, no matter what. These values were instilled in us and demanded of us as a family."

Family was first and foremost with my grandfather. He would help anyone within that circle whenever he could. It is so refreshing to know that all the things he said were based on years of experience and tradition.

My grandfather didn't say, "Do as I say." He was a "Do as I do" type of guy. He had no problem leading from the front. He strove to do the right thing and treat people the way he wanted to be treated.

Uncle Lawrence recalled, "My father shared his philosophy with anyone who wanted to do better, not just his family and friends. He was open and giving in every way."

According to Uncle Lawrence, my grandfather was never judgmental. “He let you be your own person and make your on choices. But he asked you take responsibility for your own successes and failures and not point fingers or blame others when things don’t go your way. In other words, live your life, but take responsibility for it.”

Uncle Leroy Peeler, the oldest of the siblings, described my grandfather as loving, giving, and always kind to whomever he encountered.

Aunt Mae Edith Lawson said, “My father will always live in my heart.” Her fondest memories of my grandfather were centered on his humor.

Aunt Christine Curry recalled, “He was an exceptional father and I always felt so connected to him because we shared the same birthday, September 11th.

Aunt Clementine Gunter remembered him as a symbol of courage and added, “I miss him.”

Aunt Sateria Gunter, the baby of the family, said, “As the youngest child, I experienced a lot with my father. Not all the experiences were good, but I wouldn’t change them for the world.”

Almon Gunter Sr., my father, remembered a man who knew how to get through to you. He learned an important life lesson. Never hang with a crowd – if someone does something wrong, you are guilty by association. Don’t be afraid to be alone; learn to be your own person.

My father recalled, “I know there were times he wanted to knock my head off because it appeared I wasn’t listening. But I heard every word he said. Everything he ever told me, I found to be true when I got into the real world.”

My father definitely heard my grandfather on the “don’t hang with a crowd” notion, because he instilled it in me as far back as I can remember.

My father continued, “My father helped me to be street smart. I didn’t fall in the traps that seemed to catch other people. I knew my father would be there for me if I got in trouble once, but only once. That was his rule and I knew he meant it. But he made it clear – the one time could not be for stealing or robbing, because those were things no man needed to do. Also, he wouldn’t let things go when he was talking with you. He seemed to go on forever. But everything he said was the truth, so you had to listen. He was a father of fathers.”

After listening to my grandmother, aunts, uncles, and father talk about my grandfather, I felt an incredible connection with my family. It was refreshing to know the man whom I knew, loved, and respected was all of these things to everyone he met. He shared his wisdom with each generation, in the hope it would live on.

My grandfather was my shining star – a beacon of light. This little man, who stood 5'6" and weighed roughly 130 pounds, was born in 1906, raised nine kids, experienced two world wars, the great depression, worked forty years on the railroad, and was married to my grandmother for 61 years. In 1979, he lost everything when his house burned to the ground. When the smoke cleared, he was still standing.

At a time when America was struggling with so many things, he forged his own path. He lead from the front and realized he had to create whatever he wanted. And he did!

No matter what I accomplish, it will never compare to what my grandfather endeavored. I thank him for the knowledge and wisdom he so freely shared. I thank him for instilling independence in my family and clearly defining respect, responsibility, commitment, and courage. I thank my grandfather for creating an incredible legacy.

Grandfather, we are connected by more than our last name and I love you!

FOCUS ON THE FINAL SECONDS

Journal

Focus on the Final Seconds *Journal*

Week 1: DESIRE

Desire

'The difference between a successful person and others is not a lack of strength, not a lack of knowledge, but a lack of will.'

~ Vincent Lombardi

'The spirit, the will to win and the will to excel – these are the things that endure and these are the qualities that are so much more important than any of the events that occasion them.'

~ Vincent Lombardi

'If you're lucky enough to find a guy with a lot of head and heart, he's never going to come off the field second.'

~ Vincent Lombardi

'It is essential to understand that battles are primarily won in the hearts of men. Men respond to leadership in a most remarkable way and once you have won his heart, he will follow you anywhere.'

~ Vincent Lombardi

Desire: Lead with Your Heart

Desire

- Definition – To want something with all your heart and mind.
- Identify what motivates and drives you to be your best
- To discover your passion look within yourself
- Self-image is a key element in making your dreams come true
- You possess the power to make it happen for you
- Have confidence and stick to the decisions that you make
- Lead with your heart

Use the space below to practice this week's lesson. List an example of Desire that you witnessed during the week that was either performed by you, your family, friends, neighbors, etc. For your example, please provide the Who, When, What, Where, and Why you felt that this example was appropriate.

Sunday: List one goal that you want to achieve this week.

Monday: List 5 things that you are passionate about and give an example or reason of why you are passionate about each.

Tuesday: List 5 personal strengths that will help you to keep your passion alive and ultimately help you to reach your goals.

Wednesday: What did you do today to booster your self-image and self-confidence?

Thursday: How many days this week did you meditate or allow yourself some quiet time to focus on your goals?

Friday: How many days this week did you do a physical workout that was at least 15 minutes in duration?

Saturday: Did you visualize yourself reaching your goal this week? If so, what did it look like and did you reach it?

Week 2: DEDICATION

The Hare and the Tortoise

One day the Hare was boasting, as usual, of his amazing speed. "No one can run faster than I," he bragged to the other animals. "I'm swifter than the wind.

I challenge anyone here to run a race with me."

None of the animals seemed ready to accept the challenge. "What?" said the Hare. "Will no one dare to race with me?" "I will," said a quiet voice. It was the Tortoise. "You!" the Hare exclaimed. "Surely you must be joking. How can you hope to win?" "We shall see," said the Tortoise calmly. "Let us race."

It was agreed that they would race through the woods and back. The signal was given, and the Hare hopped out of sight at once, while the Tortoise plodded slowly along.

Soon the Hare was so far ahead of the Tortoise that he stopped to rest on the soft grass. "To think that a Tortoise would want to race with me!" thought the Hare, laughing to himself. "Why, I even have time for a nap." And he curled up on the soft grass and went to sleep.

Meanwhile, the Tortoise plodded steadily on – and on and on. After a while, he passed the Hare, who was still asleep. Just as the Tortoise came to the finish line, the Hare awoke and saw where the Tortoise was. The Hare made a great leap forward, but it was too late. The Tortoise had won the race.

As the Hare crept away, shamefaced, he heard the animals exclaim, "You won! You won! How did you ever beat the Hare?"

Modestly, the Tortoise told them, "Slow and steady wins the race."

Dedication: Use Your Head

Dedication

- Definition – Committed to working hard to achieve a goal.
- Hard work comes with the program
- Give 100% effort daily
- Giving up isn't an option
- Stay your course so everyone wins
- Come early and stay late
- Commitment is a four letter word called WORK

Use the space below to practice this week's lesson. List an example of Dedication that you witnessed during the week that was either performed by you, your family, friends, neighbors, etc. For your example, please provide the Who, When, What, Where, and Why you felt that this example was appropriate.

Sunday: List one goal that you want to achieve this week.

Monday: What is your game plan for being successful this week in reaching your goal? Are you working your game plan so you can win?

Tuesday: List 5 tools that can help you to overcome obstacles in your game plan for success.

Wednesday: Are you using these 5 tools daily to help you stay the course and reach your goals? Are these tools a part of your lifestyle?

Thursday: How many days this week did you meditate or allow yourself some quiet time to focus on your goals?

Friday: How many days this week did you do a physical workout that was at least 15 minutes in duration?

Saturday: Did you visualize yourself reaching your goal this week? If so, what did it look like and did you reach it?

Week 3: DETERMINATION

Determination

'I have missed more than 9,000 shots in my career. I have lost almost 300 games. On 26 occasions I have been entrusted to take the game winning shot…and missed. And I have failed over and over again in my life. And that is why… I succeed.

- Michael Jordan

'A man can be as great as he wants to be. If you believe in yourself and have the courage, the determination, the dedication, and competitive drive and if you are willing to sacrifice the little things in life and pay the price for the things that are worthwhile, it can be done.'

- Vincent Lombardi

'Ninety-nine percent of the failures come from people who have the habit of making excuses.'

- George Washington Carver

'Far better is it to dare mighty things, to win glorious triumphs, even though checkered by failure, than to take rank with those poor spirits who neither enjoy much nor suffer much, because they live in the gray twilight that knows not victory or defeat.'

-Theodore Roosevelt

'People who soar are those who refuse to sit back, sigh and wish things would change. They neither complain of their lot nor passively dream of some distant ship coming in. Rather, they visualize in their minds that they are not quitters; they will not allow life circumstances to push them down and hold them under.'

- Charles R. Swindoll

Determination

- Definition – A fixed movement or tendency toward an object or end.
- Decide what your goals are worth to you
- Self –sacrifice is required along the way
- Be ready to rebound from a let-down
- Just because it hasn't happened, doesn't mean it won't happen
- Be willing to wait to excel – be patient and persistent
- Keep it together body, mind, and soul

Use the space below to practice this week's lesson. List an example of Determination that you witnessed during the week that was either performed by you, your family, friends, neighbors, etc. For your example, please provide the Who, When, What, Where, and Why you felt that this example was appropriate.

Sunday: List one goal that you want to achieve this week.

Monday: List the things (if any) that you are willing to give up in order to be successful in achieving your goals. (For example: negative thinking.)

Tuesday: Did you perform today to merely meet your goals or to exceed them?

Wednesday: How did you show patience and persistence this week in regards to reaching your goals?

Thursday: How many days this week did you meditate or allow yourself some quiet time to focus on your goal?

Friday: How many days this week did you do a physical workout that was at least 15 minutes in duration?

Saturday: Did you visualize yourself reaching your goal this week? If so, what did it look like and did you reach it?

Week 4: SUCCESS

SUCCESS

'Athletic sports are the great levelers, the great equators, the great melting pot. Here players are judged only on the basis of character and the ability to execute – how much they have to give and how much they are willing to give. Race, creed, and background are not important. On the playfield and in the sports arena some of the great lessons of life are practiced and learned. Selfishness and personal glory are subordinated to team effort and team glory. Here, under the white heat of emotions, players learn that to control others they must first learn to control themselves. Good is not good enough. Continuous striving for perfection is the ultimate goal, and the dedicated player will settle for nothing less. To be complacent and self-satisfied has no place in athletic sports. A player or team that is merely satisfied with winning would be satisfied to lose. Each game sets a new goal – a better performance than the preceding game. Nothing less than this will produce a winner, and winning is the American tradition, not only in sports but in all areas of life.'

~ Paul E. Brown

'I believe that when you are in any contest you should work like there is, to the very last minute, a chance to lose it.'

~ Dwight D. Eisenhower

'When prosperity comes, do not use all of it. The superior man is firm in the right way, and not merely firm.'

~ Confucius

Success: You Define the Win

- Definition – Achieving a goal that was desired, planned, or attempted by you.
- Having a dream is where success starts
- Believe you can succeed and see yourself succeeding
- Tell someone about your dream and plan to win
- Even the best plans are no good if you don't work them
- Enjoy the process
- You define the win

Use the space below to practice this week's lesson. List an example of Success being achieved that you witnessed during the week that was either performed by you, your family, friends, neighbors, etc. For your example, please provide the Who, When, What, Where, and Why you felt that this example was appropriate.

Sunday: Over the past three weeks were you successful in hitting the goals that you set?

Monday: Identify and list the tools that worked best for you over the past three weeks that allowed you to have some success.

Tuesday: Identify and list the things you want to improve upon in order for you to continue to be successful.

Wednesday: Are you stimulating and developing your body, mind, and soul on a daily basis? (How?)

Thursday: Will you continue to use meditation and or quiet time as tools to help you focus on your goals? (Why or why not?)

Friday: Will you continue to make physical fitness a part of your lifestyle? (Why or why not?)

Saturday: Will you make a commitment today to make the quantum leap and create the life you want?
(Why or why not?)

ABOUT THE AUTHOR

Almon Gunter is the CEO and President of Gunter-Gunter, Inc. He is two-time US Olympic Trial Qualifier in track and field. As a motivational speaker, author, and consultant, Almon shares his ideas, concepts, and strategies with corporations and the youth of the world, providing them with messages of passion, humor, and contagious enthusiasm.

His background provides a unique perspective on life. His love for sports, youth, and commitment to education has inspired Focus on the Final Seconds!™ The program targets individuals (adults and youth), and helps develop behaviors necessary to be successful, focused, and in control of their own destinies.

Almon believes in empowering individuals through athletics. Focus on the Final Seconds!™ is steeped in the principles of desire, dedication, and determination. His formula for success involves die-hard dedication, never-ending enthusiasm, persistent work, heart and hustle. The end result is the development of an MVP in the game of life.

ACKNOWLEDGEMENTS

To my mother, Eunice Gunter, who to this day spends many of her days and nights praying for my safe return from all of the road trips that I take. Thanks so much for just being a great mom and allowing me to spread my wings and fly. Mom, you are simply the best, and you instilled in me one of the most important lessons in winning the game of life. That lesson was to Never Quit or Give Up. And I can honestly say you have never quit on our family, your friends, and most importantly you have never quit on life. To my father, Almon W. Gunter, Sr., thanks for always letting me find my own way. You never pressured me to be anything more or less than I was and you always encouraged me to be and do my best at whatever I chose. To Brigot Gunter, thanks for all of your support and for all you do. To my children, who are the real driving force in everything that I do. It's because of each of you that I find the strength each day to carry on in my quest to build a better world. Thanks for allowing me the opportunity to be your father and know that I will always do my best for you. To my brother Dwayne and sister Amanda, I love you both. You two have always been supportive of my work and for that I say thanks. To my uncle, Lawrence Gunter, all I can say is that I love you. You have always told me I could achieve greatness even when the rest of the world said I couldn't. Thanks for believing in me from start to finish and never doubting my abilities to achieve. To the rest of my family, thanks for being so supportive, even when you didn't understand exactly what I was trying to accomplish.

To my dear childhood friends, Windell Christopher Grissett (aka Goofy), and Earriet Green (aka Easy E), we are boys for life! To Dr. David Langston and Reverend/Coach Dennis Webber, thanks for making me a part of your winning team. We might not save all the children in the world, but we are sure going to try. To Darren Burton, Thomas McCants, and Kenny Banks, I wouldn't leave you three out for the world, because you three would never let me hear the end of it. Guys, thanks for being great teammates in the game of life. And yes, sprinters are better athletes than high jumpers. To John Guidera, thanks for being a great training partner in track. We put in a ton of miles together. To Tommy Sampson and Ricky Battle, thanks for always finding the time to check up on me in all of my travels. Your friendship means a lot. Oh yeah, to my fishing partners, or should I say my band of brothers, Earriet Green (aka Easy E), Mark Collins (aka T-Bone), Nate Bryant (aka Nate the GREAT), and Tres McGibony (aka Little Brother), I will see you on the boat REEL soon! To Debbie Collins (aka Momma Debbie), and Patti Lombardo (aka Patricia L), thanks for cooking all of those great meals that kept me strong through it all.

I would also like to thank some individuals that truly helped me pull this book together: Maureen O'Meara, thanks for simply being you. You inspire me to be better. Cathy and Jeff Hurley, thanks to you both for your valuable input and feedback. Sheryl Trevino and Ty George, thanks for being a sounding board for this project and for helping me with the finishing touches. You both kicked butt on the cover and layout design of ***'Focus'***. To Dave Bell, thanks for helping me to get focused. You are the man! To Cheryl Brown, thanks for all of your suggestions and positive energy that kept me going at times. To Pat Williams, thanks for agreeing to meet with me several years ago and giving me some words of wisdom that in many ways changed my life. To Dr. Lisa Williams, I will never forget you and your input. Your presence forced me to raise the bar even higher and I am eternally grateful. To Alisa Hunt, thanks for being supportive and for providing such valuable input. To Yvette Arline, I will always treasure your friendship and thanks for writing the foreword for this book and supporting my efforts. There are so many others that I would like to thank in this acknowledgement because of their love and support, but I don't want to risk leaving anyone out so I will just say thanks to all of my remaining friends and supporters. You know who you are.

Finally, I would like to say thanks to the man who showed me the way, my grandfather Wilson Gunter. Without your love, support, and guidance, I would not be half the man I am today. Thanks for the life lessons you taught me and the tough love you showed when necessary. Your love, guidance, and spirit are with me always. Thanks for leaving a legacy of education, honor, love, and peace. I will do my best to always live and not merely exist so I may have the opportunity to inspire others, as you have inspired me. Thanks for providing me with the tools necessary to reach my Maximum Velocity Performance. Because of you, I could compete in and win the Game of Life! You will always be the wind beneath my wings!

For more information on other products by
Almon W. Gunter, Jr.

KEYNOTES
BOOKS
TRAINING CAMPS
CONSULTING

Please Contact Gunter-Gunter, Inc.
Post Office Box 194
Jacksonville, FL 32234
Phone: 904.565.2911
Fax: 904.266.3216

Website: www.guntergunterinc.com

Via-email
Almon@guntergunterinc.com

Give GGI a call today

So you can
Focus on the Final Seconds!™
and Win the Game of Life!

www.ingramcontent.com/pod-product-compliance
Lightning Source LLC
Chambersburg PA
CBHW020508100426
42813CB00030B/3158/J

* 9 7 8 1 5 9 9 3 2 0 2 6 7 *